The Best of MAILBOX Ma...
Caterpillars & Butterflies

MW00668572

Our best caterpillar and butterfly activities and reproducibles from the 1998–2011 issues of *The Mailbox* and *Teacher's Helper* magazines

- **Literacy activities**

- **Learning centers**

- **Group-time activities**

- **Songs, poems, and fingerplays**

- **Math activities**

- **Arts-and-crafts ideas**

- **...and more!**

Fun and practical skills practice!

Managing Editor: Brenda Fay

Editorial Team: Becky S. Andrews, Diane Badden, Kimberley Bruck, Karen A. Brudnak, Pam Crane, Chris Curry, David Drews, Tazmen Fisher Hansen, Marsha Heim, Lori Z. Henry, Mark Rainey, Greg D. Rieves, Hope Rodgers-Medina, Rebecca Saunders, Donna K. Teal, Sharon M. Tresino, Michele D. Warta, Zane Williard

www.themailbox.com

©2013 The Mailbox® Books
All rights reserved.
ISBN 978-1-61276-370-5

Printed in the United States
10 9 8 7 6 5 4 3 2 1

HPS246109

Table of Contents

Literacy Fun With Butterfly Friends!

These butterfly-themed literacy activities are just perfect for little learners!

🦋 /b/, /b/, Butterfly! 🦋

Recognizing matching sounds

Give each child a construction paper butterfly cutout (pattern on page 5). Provide items with names that begin with /b/, such as a small plastic bottle, blocks, a small ball, a plastic toy bear, a gift bow, and a banana. Place the objects near shallow pans of paint. A youngster chooses an item and says its name. Then she says the word *butterfly,* noticing that the two words begin with the same sound. She dips the object in the paint and then presses it on or drags it across the butterfly. She continues with the remaining objects until a desired effect is achieved.

Roxanne LaBell Dearman, Western NC Early Intervention Program for Children Who Are Deaf or Hard of Hearing, Charlotte, NC

🦋 Which Character? 🦋

Recalling book events

Read aloud the story *Bob and Otto* by Robert O. Bruel. In the story, Bob the caterpillar and Otto the earthworm are friends. But when Bob becomes a butterfly, Otto feels boring and useless. After the read-aloud, give each student a strip of pink paper (Otto) and a strip of orange paper (Bob). Have each child make blue stripes on the orange strip so it further resembles Bob. Name a story event. (See the suggestions below.) Then have youngsters hold up the critter that corresponds to the event. Continue with each remaining event.

Suggested events:
He climbs a tree.
He goes into the ground.
He digs under the tree.
He eats fresh, green leaves.
He eats rotten, old leaves.
He falls asleep on a branch.
He loves to dig.
He turns into a butterfly.
He says, "Why are you sad?"

🦋 Metamorphosis of Me 🦋
Writing

To make this adorable display, take a photo of each child wrapped in a green blanket so it appears as if she is a chrysalis. Help each child cut out her photo. Then display the photos upside down as shown. Prompt each child to say what she would be thinking if she were waiting to turn into a butterfly. Then write her words on a thought bubble and attach it near her photo. The next week, have her remove her chrysalis photo and attach it to a butterfly cutout (pattern on page 5). Have her decorate the wings as desired. Then display the butterflies with new dictation.

Danielle Rieth, The World Schools, Nashua, NH

When I'm a butterfly, I will be really pretty with big wings.

I can fly really high up in the air.

🦋 Bow Tie Butterflies 🦋
Identifying the letter B

Place bow tie pasta (farfalle) in a resealable plastic bag. Add a small amount of rubbing alcohol and food coloring. Then seal the bag and shake it to evenly distribute the coloring. (Add more coloring and alcohol, if needed.) Spread the pasta on a piece of waxed paper to dry overnight. Next, give each child a copy of page 6 and several pieces of pasta (butterflies). Have him glue a butterfly to each *B* on the page. *B* is for butterfly!

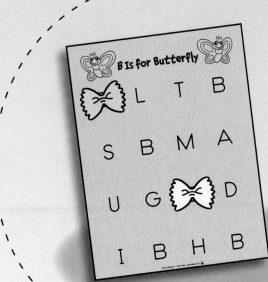

Editor's Tip:

These bow tie butterflies are also fabulous for arts and crafts. Have each student draw flowers on a sheet of paper. Then encourage him to glue bow tie butterflies around the flowers. Now that's a simple and cute craft!

🦋 Let's Fly! 🦋
Identifying letters, matching letters

Make a letter card for each letter in *butterfly*. Give each card to a child. Write the letter *b* on your board and help students identify the letter. Then prompt the child with the *b* card to "fly" to the front of the room. Continue with each remaining letter in the word until youngsters are lined up appropriately with their letter cards. Finally, have students hold up their cards as you read the word aloud.

Marie E. Cecchini, West Dundee, IL

Butterfly Pattern

Use with "/b/, /b/, Butterfly!" on page 3, "Metamorphosis of Me" on page 4; and "Tie-Dye Butterfly" on page 30.

TEC61385

 # B Is for Butterfly

B L T B

S B M A

U G B D

I B H B

Caterpillars & Butterflies • ©The Mailbox® Books • TEC61385

Note to the teacher: Use with "Bow Tie Butterflies" on page 4.

Up and Down

Little ones will be all aflutter with butterfly-themed ideas that help teach the concepts of *up* and *down*.

ideas by Lucia Kemp Henry

Butterflies in Motion

What makes this activity about up and down so appealing to pre-schoolers? A catchy song and a crafty butterfly that moves like the real thing! Have each child create his own model butterfly by using a glue stick to attach a pair of tissue paper wings to a craft stick as shown. Then gather your students together with their butterflies. Have each child use his thumb and index finger to hold one end of the craft stick. Demonstrate how to gently move the butterfly up and down so the tissue paper wings flutter. After students have practiced flying their but-terflies, sing the song below and direct each child to move his butterfly as directed in the song. *fine-motor skills, positional words, singing simple songs*

(sung to the tune of "London Bridge")

Butterflies fly **up** and **down**,
Up and **down**,
Up and **down**.
Butterflies fly **up** and **down**!
See them flutter.

They flap their wings
And **up** they go!
Up they go!
Up they go!
They flap their wings
And **up** they go!
See them flutter.

Gently, softly,
Down they come.
Down they come.
Down they come.
Gently, softly,
Down they come.
See them flutter.

Pulling Strings

How do you get these crafty butterflies to fly? It's easy! Just pull some strings! Have each child decorate a tagboard butterfly shape. Then punch a hole in the top of the shape and tie a 24-inch length of string through the hole. Next, use a pencil to poke a hole in the bottom of a six-ounce paper cup. Thread the string through the hole as shown and then tie a small bead to the end of the string. Gently pull and release the string to move the butterfly up and down. Have the child use her butterfly craft to act out the song in "Butterflies in Motion" or to play the game described in "Simon Says, 'Going Up!'" on page 8. *positional words, fine-motor skills*

Simon Says, "Going Up!"

Reinforce a variety of preschool skills with this adaptation of Simon Says. Provide each child with the butterfly craft described in "Pulling Strings" on page 7. Have students practice moving the butterflies up and down. Then give students simple directions such as "Simon says, 'Move your butterflies *up.*'" Gradually increase the level of difficulty by adding to the directions. For example, you might say, "Simon says, '*Slowly* move your butterflies up'" or "Simon says, 'Move your butterflies down *a little.*'" When students are familiar with the activity, invite a child to stand in front of the class and take a turn leading a round of Simon Says. *fine-motor skills, positional words, following directions, vocabulary*

Butterfly, I Spy

Get ready for some camouflage fun with this activity about up and down, which also sharpens visual discrimination skills. To begin, prepare a felt scene on your flannelboard similar to the one shown. Then cut out a supply of butterflies (patterns on page 9) from white, green, and blue felt. During your group time, turn the flannelboard away from students' view and place the white butterflies on the cloud. Turn the board back around and invite students to participate in the call-and-response rhyme below. After reciting the rhyme, invite a child to remove the camouflaged butterflies from the board. Continue the activity in a similar manner, hiding the blue butterflies *down* in the water, and the green butterflies *down* in the grass and then *up* in the tree. *visual discrimination, positional words, language development*

Teacher: Do you spy some butterflies?
Students: Yes, we do with our sharp little eyes.
Teacher: Where can all those butterflies be?
Students: [Up] in the [clouds]! It's easy to see!

TEC61385

TEC61385

TEC61385

TEC61385

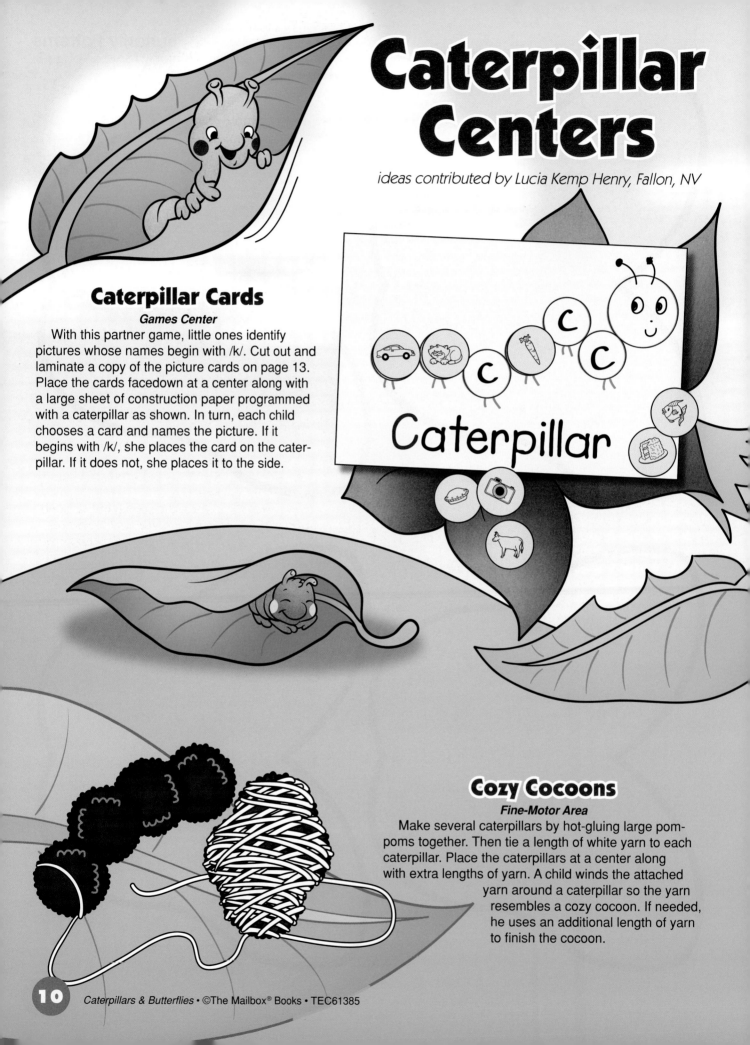

Caterpillar Centers

ideas contributed by Lucia Kemp Henry, Fallon, NV

Caterpillar Cards

Games Center

With this partner game, little ones identify pictures whose names begin with /k/. Cut out and laminate a copy of the picture cards on page 13. Place the cards facedown at a center along with a large sheet of construction paper programmed with a caterpillar as shown. In turn, each child chooses a card and names the picture. If it begins with /k/, she places the card on the caterpillar. If it does not, she places it to the side.

Cozy Cocoons

Fine-Motor Area

Make several caterpillars by hot-gluing large pompoms together. Then tie a length of white yarn to each caterpillar. Place the caterpillars at a center along with extra lengths of yarn. A child winds the attached yarn around a caterpillar so the yarn resembles a cozy cocoon. If needed, he uses an additional length of yarn to finish the cocoon.

Munchin' Lunch

Writing Center

In advance, make a class supply of simple accordion booklets. Label the cover of each booklet as shown. Then place the booklets at a center along with scissors and grocery store circulars. Read aloud *The Very Hungry Caterpillar* by Eric Carle. Then invite youngsters to visit the center. A student draws a caterpillar at the top of the first page. Then he cuts out pictures of food and attaches one picture to each page. He dictates the names of the food items for an adult helper to write in his booklet. That's one hungry caterpillar!

Colorful Caterpillar

Art Center

Place shallow pans of paint at a table along with a round sponge and cotton swab for each pan. A youngster makes several sponge prints on a sheet of paper so they resemble a caterpillar. She uses a cotton swab to make spots on her caterpillar. When the paint is dry, she draws a mouth on her project and attaches hole reinforcer eyes and pipe cleaner antennae and feet.

Scrumptious Leaves

Science Center

This cute idea reinforces that caterpillars eat leaves. Place at a table construction paper leaf cutouts (pattern on page 14), copies of page 15, three-inch pieces of flexible drinking straws (include the flexible portion), a hole puncher, and glue. A visiting child tears small pieces of paper from the edges of a leaf so it looks as if it's been nibbled on; then she punches several holes in the leaf. Next, she glues the leaf to a sheet of paper. Then she shapes the straw so it resembles a caterpillar and glues it to the leaf.

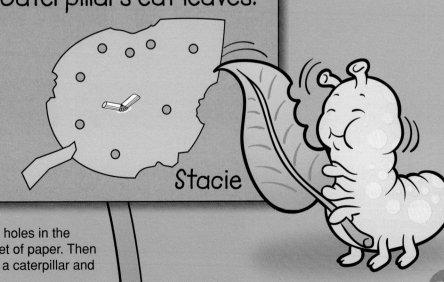

Caterpillar Names

Literacy Center

For each child, write each letter of her name on a separate circle cutout. Put the circles plus a circle decorated with a caterpillar face in a personalized envelope. Place the envelopes at a center. A visiting youngster locates her envelope and removes the circles. She places the caterpillar head on a flat surface. Then she arranges the circles next to the head to spell her name, using her envelope as a guide. If desired, she repeats the process with her classmates' names.

Andrea Singleton, Waynesville Elementary
Waynesville, OH

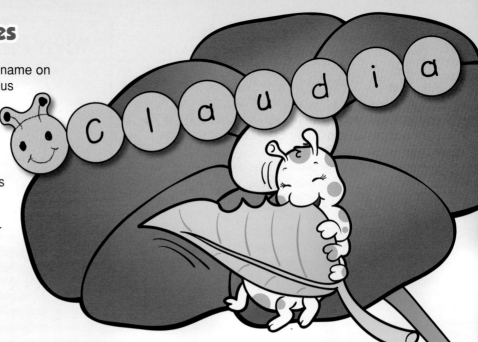

Lots of Caterpillars!

Math Center

Youngsters practice identifying numbers and making sets with this idea. Place a supersize leaf cutout at a center along with bingo daubers. Attach a number card to the leaf. A little one identifies the number and then uses the bingo daubers to make caterpillars with the corresponding number of body segments on the leaf. For an added challenge, change the leaf and number card each day.

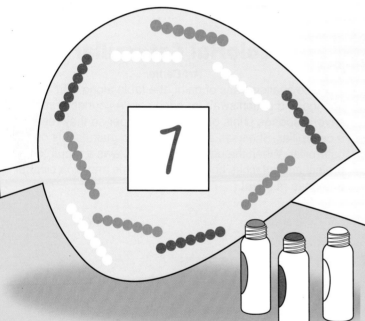

Very Hungry Caterpillars

Play Dough Center

To prepare for this center, make a supersize caterpillar cutout (pattern on page 16). Place the caterpillar at the center along with play dough and rolling pins. A visiting child uses the items to make food for the caterpillar; then she pretends to feed it. What a delicious looking caterpillar feast!

TEC61385

TEC61385

TEC61385

TEC61385

TEC61385

TEC61385

TEC61385

TEC61385

Leaf Pattern

Use with "Scrumptious Leaves" on page 11 and "Pom-Pom Pals" on page 30.

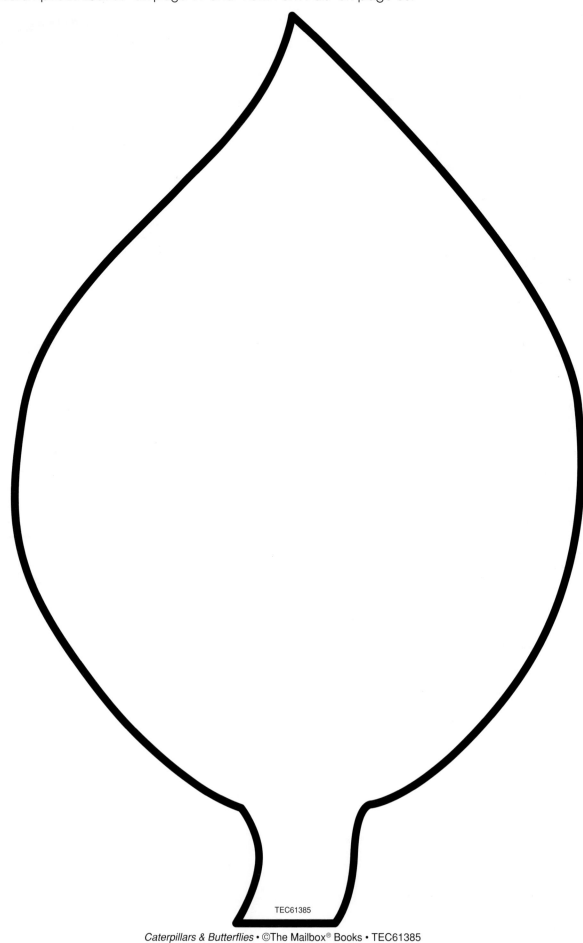

TEC61385

Name _____

Caterpillars eat leaves.

Caterpillars & Butterflies • ©The Mailbox® Books • TEC61385

Note to the teacher: Use with "Scrumptious Leaves" on page 11.

15

Caterpillar Pattern

Use with "Very Hungry Caterpillars" on page 12.

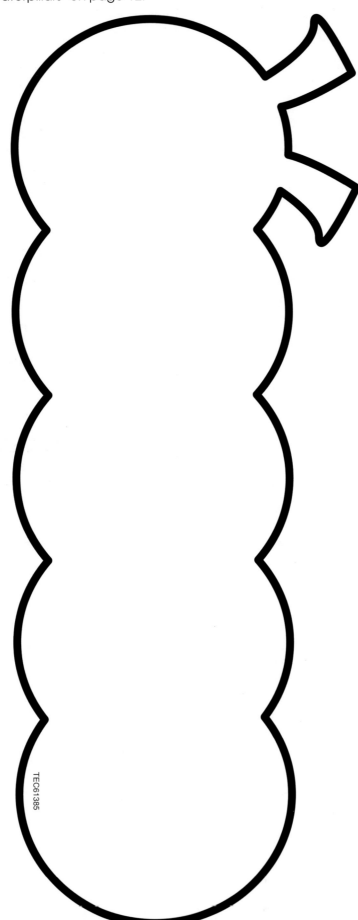

TEC61385

THE VERY
HUNGRY
CATERPILLAR
by Eric Carle

The Very Hungry Caterpillar

Written and Illustrated by Eric Carle

Join a ravenous caterpillar as he eats his way through the days of the week. By Saturday he has eaten so much he has a tummyache. But the caterpillar knows what to do. He eats a leaf and spins a chrysalis, and two weeks later he emerges as a beautiful butterfly!

ideas by Suzanne Moore, Irving, TX

Caterpillar Lotto

Children delight in playing this lively lotto game featuring the foods the caterpillar eats in the story. To prepare the game for two players, make two white construction paper copies of the gameboards on pages 19 and 20. Color the pages so that the same foods are the same colors. Then cut out the food pictures from one copy of each page to make playing cards. To play, give each player a gameboard, shuffle the cards, and then place the cards facedown in a stack. The first child takes a card from the top of the stack. If he has a matching food on his board, he puts the card on top of it. If he does not have a match, he returns his card to the bottom of the pile. Play alternates between players until both students have covered their boards. Lotto!

Feed the Caterpillar

Youngsters have fun feeding this always hungry caterpillar. In advance, make a copy of pages 19 and 20. Color the pictures, and then cut out the food picture cards (or use the cards made for "Caterpillar Lotto" on this page). Next, create a caterpillar by covering a cylindrical oatmeal or raisin container with green construction paper. Cut a mouth in the plastic lid and glue construction paper eyes and antennae to the lid to create a caterpillar face. To play, have each child mix up the food cards and then retell the story by slipping each food card into the caterpillar's mouth in order. Munch, munch!

Where Will You Fly?

This simple bulletin board project will really spark students' imaginations. Ask children to brainstorm where the butterfly goes after the book ends; accept all student suggestions. Next, have each child cut several colors of tissue paper into small pieces. Then have her fill a snack-size resealable plastic bag with the pieces. Seal her bag and then twist a pipe cleaner around the middle of the bag to create antennae. Staple each child's butterfly to a piece of 9" x 12" blue construction paper. Then have the child draw to show where the butterfly might go. Write her dictation on her paper. Mount the completed projects on a bulletin board titled "Where Will You Fly?"

The butterfly will fly to the park.
Macy

Making Changes

Revisit *The Very Hungry Caterpillar* with your students, pointing out some of the stages of a butterfly's life cycle. Explain that a butterfly starts out as an egg, becomes a caterpillar, forms a chrysalis, and then becomes a butterfly. Then set up this simple art center to reinforce the sequence of a butterfly's life cycle. In advance, dye a supply of large pasta shells with dye made by mixing brown food coloring paste with rubbing alcohol. (You can also combine red and green food coloring to make brown, but the color will not be as vibrant.) You'll also need to dye a supply of bow-tie pasta red, yellow, and blue in the same way. Stock a center with a class supply of colored paper plates, each of which has been divided into four sections. Also supply glue, dry orzo, and uncooked rigatoni, along with the dyed pasta. Explain that the orzo represents the egg, the rigatoni represents the caterpillar, the large shell represents the chrysalis, and the bow-tie pasta represents the butterfly. Make a sample of the completed project to display for correct sequencing of the life cycle. Then have each student glue the items representing the different stages of the life cycle in sequential order on her plate. Ah, the life of a butterfly!

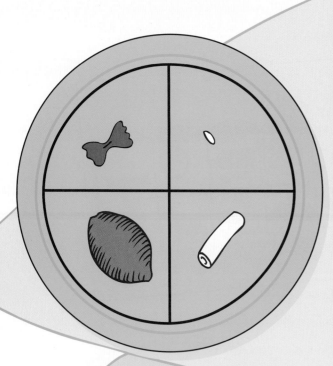

Caterpillar Snack

Students are ready to munch when they make and eat this fun caterpillar snack! Provide each child with a scoop of canned fruit cocktail and a straw. Have him use the straw to pierce each fruit piece, making a hole just like the ones the caterpillar makes. Then invite each child to eat his fruity snack!

Caterpillar Lotto

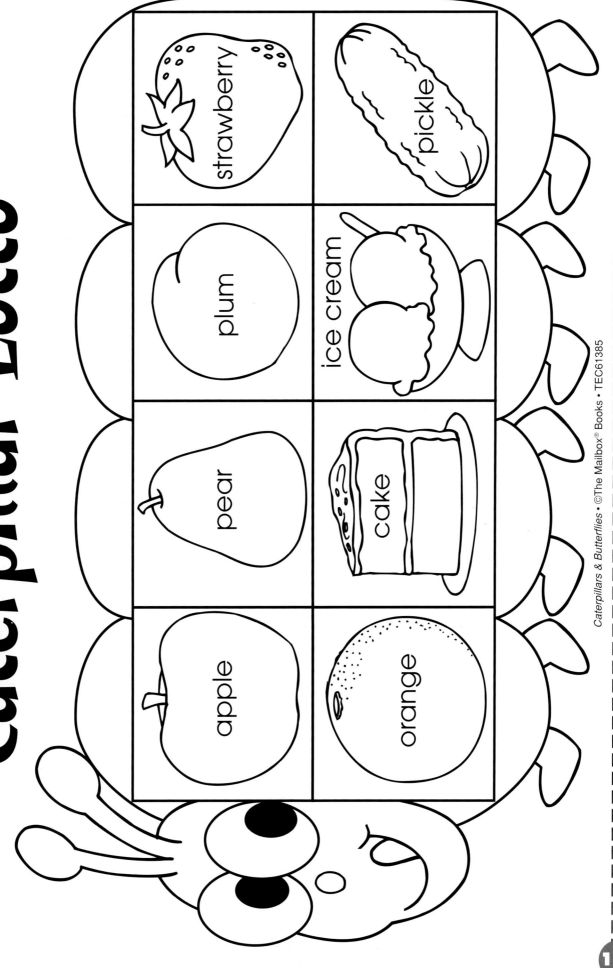

| strawberry | plum | pear | apple |
| pickle | ice cream | cake | orange |

Caterpillars & Butterflies • ©The Mailbox® Books • TEC61385

Note to the teacher: Use with "Caterpillar Lotto" and "Feed the Caterpillar" on page 17.

Caterpillar Lotto

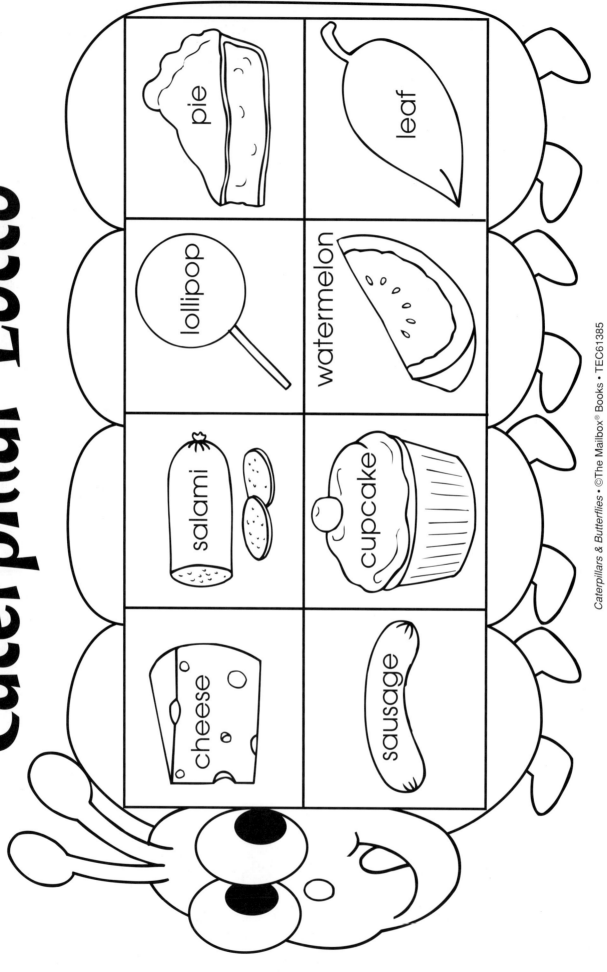

pie	leaf
lollipop	watermelon
salami	cupcake
cheese	sausage

Caterpillars & Butterflies • ©The Mailbox® Books • TEC61385

Note to the teacher: Use with "Caterpillar Lotto" and "Feed the Caterpillar" on page 17.

The Wonder Of Butterflies

What's that flitting and fluttering around gardens and backyards? The beautiful butterfly, of course! Introduce your little ones to this graceful creature with these activities. They'll be all aflutter over butterflies!

ideas contributed by Marie E. Cecchini

Butterfly Journeys

Ask your youngsters to close their eyes and pretend that they are butterflies. Read aloud the poem "If I Were A Butterfly." After sharing the poem, have the children open their eyes. Invite them to use colored chalk and large sheets of drawing paper to draw a picture that answers the question, "Where would you go if you were a butterfly?" Set the mood for this activity by playing soft, instrumental music as the children work. Encourage your youngsters to use their fingers to blend the colors of chalk to create soft effects in their drawings. (Keep a supply of moist towelettes handy for easy cleanup.) Write as each child dictates a sentence about her imaginary journey.

Write the poem on a large butterfly shape cut from bulletin-board paper. Display the poem along with the children's daydreamlike drawings. To complete the display, add the title "Butterfly Journeys." Beautiful!

If I Were A Butterfly

If I were a butterfly,
Then no one would know
Wherever it was
I decided to go.

I could visit a farm,
A lake, or a zoo.
You just never know
What it is I might do.

Maybe I'd flit
From flower to flower
Drawing up nectar
To drink by the hour.

I might like to go
To the park or the beach,
Or soar to the sky
Where no one could reach.

I think I would like it,
At least I would try.
But I don't have wings
Like a butterfly.

—Marie E. Cecchini

I would fly near all the grass.

The Beginnings Of A Butterfly

Your little ones will be fascinated to learn about the growth cycle of the butterfly. Share a nonfiction book about butterfly growth, such as *Monarch Butterfly* by Gail Gibbons. As youngsters view the pictures, paraphrase the text to suit your students' interest level.

After discussing the growth cycle of a butterfly, prepare a sheet of chart paper with the story-starter sentence, "Once upon a time, there was a little egg." Ask the children to help you write a story about the growth of a butterfly. Personalize the story by naming the caterpillar in your tale. When the story has taken your caterpillar character from egg to butterfly, reread it to the class and invite them to share their comments. Display the story on a wall or bulletin board.

Then invite students to become illustrators as well as authors. Give each child a turn at a painting easel that is supplied with large sheets of art paper and several colors of paint. Have each child paint her favorite part of the caterpillar's story. When everyone has had an opportunity to create an illustration, mount the finished artwork around the chart story.

Counting Caterpillars

What could be more fun than a wriggly rhyme? Create a pair of storytelling gloves to wear that will delight your youngsters as you tell this tale of metamorphosis. Purchase a pair of canvas work gloves. Paint the palms of the gloves with bright colors of fabric paint; then allow the paint to dry thoroughly. To the top of each glove's fingertips, attach the hook side of a small piece of self-adhesive Velcro®. Prepare the eggs by attaching the loop side of a piece of Velcro® to each of five small, white pom-poms. To prepare each of the caterpillars, use hot glue to attach four small, green pom-poms together. Hot glue two wiggle eyes to one end of each caterpillar. Attach the loop side of a piece of Velcro® to the underside of each caterpillar. Attach each egg to the left glove and each caterpillar to the right glove. Put on the gloves; then follow the directions to make this story come to life!

Five Little Caterpillars

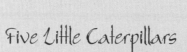

Five little eggs Sitting on a leaf. Will they ever hatch? Oh my! Good grief!	*Hide right fingers under left hand.*	Three little caterpillars Wondering what to do. One crawls away, And then there are two.	*Remove caterpillar from middle finger.*
Then before you know it, Quick as a wink, Out come caterpillars— Five, I think.	*Extend and wiggle fingers of right hand.* *Count "1-2-3-4-5."*	Two little caterpillars Just having fun. One crawls away, And then there is one.	*Remove caterpillar from index finger.*
They're eating and eating And eating some more. One crawls away, And then there are four.	*Wiggle fingers.* *Remove caterpillar from pinky.*	One little caterpillar… Now, what's this? Just like magic, He's formed a chrysalis!	*Wrap fingers around thumb.*
Four little caterpillars Happy as can be. One crawls away, And then there are three.	*Remove caterpillar from ring finger.*	Just watch and see. Don't blink an eye. The chrysalis opens. He's become a butterfly!	*Remove caterpillar from thumb.* *Lock thumbs; extend and wiggle fingers.*

—Marie E. Cecchini

Spread Your Wings

Encourage your little ones to dramatize the metamorphosis of an egg into a butterfly with this movement activity. Before beginning the activity, make a pair of butterfly wings for each child. To make a pair of wings, simply gather a large sheet of colorful tissue paper in the center and secure it with a spring-type clothespin. Set the wings aside for students to use at the end of the activity.

To begin, invite each child to pretend that she is an unhatched caterpillar, curled tightly inside an egg. Ask each child to "hatch" from her egg. Then encourage each wiggling, hungry caterpillar to crawl about, search for food, and "munch" on her favorite plants. When each caterpillar decides she is so full she can hardly move, have her pretend to form a chrysalis. Then visit each "sleeping" caterpillar to clip a pair of butterfly wings to the back of her clothing. When each caterpillar has received her wings, tell her to begin "breaking" from her chrysalis. Encourage each little butterfly to crawl out of her chrysalis, then rest as her wings dry and stretch out in the sun. Invite the newborn butterflies to "fly" gently around the room and out to the playground. Fly away!

adapted from an idea by Marsha Feffer—Pre-K
Salem Early Childhood Center
Salem, MA

Barefoot Butterflies

Let these butterflies do a graceful two-step across your classroom walls! Begin by spreading newspaper over a tabletop and the surrounding floor area. Working with one student at a time, ask each child to remove his shoe and sock from one foot. Use a paintbrush to cover the bottom of the child's foot with a bright color of washable paint. Then have him press a footprint onto the center of a 12" x 18" sheet of white drawing paper. (Have a tub of warm water and some paper towels handy for immediate cleanup.) Have the child replace his sock and shoe. Using several different colors of washable paint, paint the palms and fingers of both his hands. Ask him to make a set of handprints on each side of the footprint. Then instruct him to wash and dry his hands. Allow the footprint and handprints to dry. When the paint is dry, have each child cut around the shape of his butterfly. Give each child two wiggle eyes to glue onto his butterfly. Tape two pipe-cleaner antennae to the butterfly. Then invite each child to flutter his butterfly to a chosen spot on a classroom wall. Use masking tape to mount the butterflies in place for a springtime parade!

Kathleen Lademan—Pre-K
Noah's Ark Child Care Center, Portland, ME

Explorations

Crazy About Caterpillars

Woolly or smooth. Green or spotted. Caterpillars of all varieties are fascinating to children. Follow these directions to make a caterpillar cage. Find your own caterpillar to temporarily inhabit the cage, or order caterpillars online. The opportunity to observe firsthand the metamorphosis of a butterfly (or moth) is an experience your preschoolers will never forget.

Before you begin, contact a local entomology expert for information about common caterpillars in your area. Mention that you are hoping to find a caterpillar with a short pupal stage.

Cut one or more windows in the carton. Place the twig and some leaves inside.

Slide the carton very carefully into the hosiery leg. Pull the hose nearly all the way up the carton.

In about two weeks,* your caterpillar may spin a cocoon, if it's a moth…

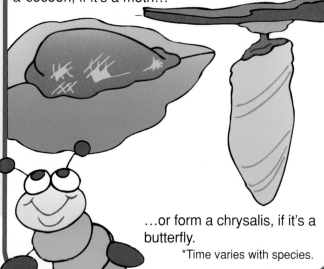

…or form a chrysalis, if it's a butterfly.

*Time varies with species.

About two weeks later,* a moth or butterfly will emerge.

Keep the butterfly (or moth) for only a day. Then release it.

*Time varies with species.

Science You Can Do *by Ann Flagg*

To make a caterpillar cage, you will need:
— a clean, empty half-gallon carton
— scissors
— one leg of nylon hosiery
— a twig
— some leaves (preferably the kind of leaves you find your caterpillar on)
— a journal (optional)

Find a caterpillar and put it in your caterpillar cage.

Stretch the hose up over the top of the carton and knot it to close the cage.

Make regular entries in a journal to document what happens to the caterpillar.

Every day remove the old leaves and waste; then provide fresh leaves for your caterpillar. It will get the water it needs from the fresh leaves.

Did You Know?

- Butterflies lay eggs that are so tiny we usually do not see them.
- After a caterpillar hatches from one of the eggs, it begins to eat many times its own body weight daily.
- Because a caterpillar eats so much, it grows rapidly. It sheds its skin to accommodate the growth.
- A caterpillar lives for at least two weeks before becoming a pupa. It will attach itself to a sheltered spot and form a hard shell, called a *chrysalis*. This stage may last from just a few days to more than a year.
- The chrysalis cracks when the adult butterfly has formed. The butterfly then frees itself.
- One or two weeks is the length of time most butterflies live. But some live up to 18 months.

What Now?

- Read *The Very Hungry Caterpillar* by Eric Carle. Talk about what is real and what is make-believe in this story.

- Clean out your caterpillar cage. Replace the twig and leaves. Then find a different creature to inhabit the cage for a day. Now where did that ladybug go?

More Caterpillar

A Colorful Caterpillar
Number order

Enlist youngsters' help in getting this cute caterpillar in order. Make several numbered circle cutouts. On the floor, place a caterpillar head cutout (pattern on page 40). Distribute the numbered circles. Ask the student with circle 1 to place it beside the caterpillar's head. Direct the child with the next circle to place it beside the first circle. Continue until the caterpillar's body is complete. Lead little ones in counting the numbers on the caterpillar's body to check the accuracy of the number order.

Sharon Berkley, Son Shine Christian Preschool
Pasadena, TX

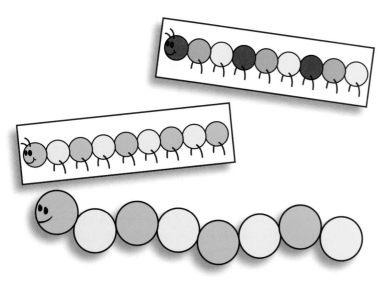

Caterpillar Patterns
Copying and extending patterns

In advance, use sticky dots to make several different pattern cards (cards on page 41). Provide a supply of corresponding-colored die-cut circles for each pattern, programming one circle so it resembles a caterpillar's head. A student chooses a caterpillar pattern card. Then she arranges the circles to copy and extend the pattern.

Leslie Curran
Play Groups
East Setauket, NY

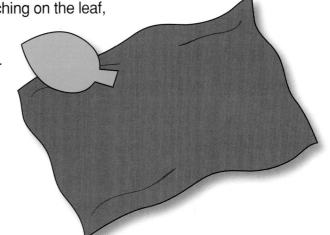

From Caterpillar to Butterfly
Dramatizing a song

After youngsters are familiar with the life cycle of a butterfly, lead them in singing the song shown. Next, invite a volunteer to act out the song. Provide her with a green paper leaf and a small blanket (chrysalis) to wrap herself in. Then lead youngsters in singing the song again. As the group sings, prompt the child to act out crawling like a caterpillar, munching on the leaf, forming a chrysalis, and then flying away as a beautiful butterfly. Invite other students to act out the song; then put the props in a center for independent use.

(sung to the tune of "Clementine")

Caterpillar, caterpillar,
Eating leaves and crawling round;
You are big and so you make a
Chrysalis far off the ground.

Caterpillar, caterpillar,
You are such a big surprise.
You have wings and you're so lovely!
Oh, I can't believe my eyes.

Be a Butterfly!
Life cycle of a butterfly

At this center, youngsters transform themselves from a caterpillar into a beautiful butterfly! To prepare, place several leaf cutouts, a sleeping bag, and two colorful scarves at a center. Also attach several flower cutouts to the floor in an open area. A child pretends to be a caterpillar, crawling on the floor and munching on leaves. Then he crawls inside the sleeping bag (chrysalis) and pretends to sleep. After a short rest, he emerges from the sleeping bag with a colorful scarf in each hand (butterfly wings). Then he flies around gathering nectar from the flowers.

Angie Martin
Angie's Angels Childcare
Roxboro, NC

Beautiful Butterflies
Fine-motor skills

Provide an assortment of colorful fabric squares along with plastic spring-style clothespins. A youngster gathers a fabric square and then grasps the center of the gathered material with a clothespin. He gently "flies" the resulting butterfly around the room.

Fluffy Caterpillars
Fine-motor skills

Cut out an oversize leaf shape and place it on the floor in a traffic-free area. Place a container of pom-poms in assorted sizes and colors next to the leaf. A child arranges the pom-poms on the leaf to make caterpillars in a variety of unique sizes and color combinations.

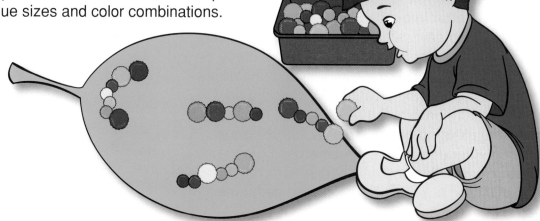

Handsome Butterflies
Art

Attach several of these butterflies to a wall in your classroom to make an eye-catching display. Have each youngster press both of her hands in a shallow container of paint and then make handprints, as shown, that resemble a butterfly. Next, trim the student's head from a photograph. Instruct her to glue the head cutout above the wings. Then have her use a permanent marker to add details to the butterfly, such as antennae. That's one unique butterfly!

Kimberly Hernandez
Dunbar Early Childhood Education Center
Wichita, KS

Caterpillar Note Holder
Art

These caterpillar clips make perfect gifts. To make a caterpillar clip, glue six small pom-poms on top of a spring-type clothespin. Glue a medium-size pom-pom to the upper end of the clothespin. When it is firmly in place, glue two small wiggle eyes to it. This makes a great clip for holding message slips, grocery lists, or coupons.

Michele Melson, Cartersville, GA

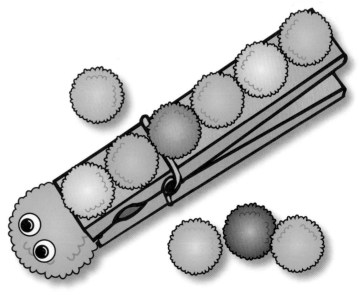

Pom-Pom Pals
Art

Brighten your classroom with these colorful caterpillars! To begin, make a green leaf cutout (pattern on page 14) and then use fancy-edged scissors to cut a bite shape from the leaf. Draw a line on the leaf and then squeeze glue on the line. Place a row of colorful pom-poms on the glue to resemble a caterpillar. If desired, glue construction paper eyes and antennae to the caterpillar. When the glue is dry, display the leaves on a tree shape cut from bulletin board paper.

Lisa Migliaccio
Buffalo Hearing and Speech Center
Buffalo, NY

Tie-Dye Butterfly
Process art

To make a butterfly, put a generous amount of nonmentholated shaving cream on a tray. Use eyedroppers to drip different colors of diluted paint onto the shaving cream; then blend the colors into the shaving cream using a craft stick. Next, press a butterfly cutout (pattern on page 5) on the shaving cream; then lift the paper from the tray. Finally, use the side of the craft stick to gently remove the excess shaving cream from the paper.

Misty Moesser
North Park Elementary
North Logan, UT

Clay Creations
Art

Explore the shapes and colors of caterpillars and butterflies with this sculpting and painting activity. Have the children assist in preparing a batch of baker's dough using the recipe provided. Give each child a small amount of dough. Ask her to begin by pulling off a ball of dough and rolling it into a caterpillar. Then have her use a small rolling pin to flatten the remainder of her dough. Provide a butterfly-shaped cookie cutter and ask each child to cut a butterfly from her dough. Place the shapes on waxed-paper-covered cookie sheets. Use a permanent marker to print each child's name on the waxed paper next to her shapes. Bake the children's creations in a 300˚ oven for 30 to 60 minutes or until dry. When the shapes have cooled, provide paints and brushes for students to decorate their clay figures.

Baker's Dough
(enough for approximately 16 students)

2 cups flour
1 cup salt
¾ cup water
Mix all the ingredients together, adding additional water if necessary.
Knead until the mixture forms a smooth dough.

Drizzle Butterfly
Process art

Spring fancy takes flight on the wings of these giant butterflies. To make one of these dazzlers, cut a giant butterfly shape from bulletin board paper. Place the cutout on a protected tabletop. Using water, thin three to four pastel colors of paint. If a semigloss look is desired, rather than a flat look, add some white glue to the thinned paint. Then dip a brush in one color of paint and allow the liquid to drizzle onto the butterfly cutout as you move the brush around several inches off the surface of the paper. Repeat the drizzling process using additional brushes and two or three other colors of paint.

Linda Schwitzke, Headstart, Longview, WA

Beautiful Butterfly

No doubt your little ones will giggle with glee when they sing this silly little ditty!

(sung to the tune of "O Christmas Tree")

Oh butterfly, oh butterfly,
Your wings are all aflutter.
Oh butterfly, oh butterfly,
Which part of you is butter?
There is no butter, I can see,
On this small critter wild and free.
Oh butterfly, oh butterfly,
Your wings are all aflutter.

Vicki Padgett
Arlington Baptist Church Preschool
Charlotte, NC

BUTTER

Crunching Caterpillar

The caterpillar in this song will munch on just about anything! Lead youngsters in singing the song. Then have a child volunteer the name of a food. Have students repeat the song, inserting the name of the new food when indicated. Continue in the same way for several rounds.

(sung to the tune of "Did You Ever See a Lassie?")

Did you ever see a caterpillar, a caterpillar, a caterpillar?
Did you ever see a caterpillar chew on a [leaf]?
He'll crunch, crunch, crunch, crunch, crunch,
And munch, munch, munch, munch, munch.
Did you ever see a caterpillar chew on a [leaf]?

Sue Fleischmann
Sussex, WI

From Caterpillar to Butterfly

Brighten a study of butterflies with this informative chant!

I'm a caterpillar so cute and green.
I'm inside a chrysalis and can't be seen.
Wait a little while and you will see why.
I'll pop out as a butterfly!

Wiggle pointer finger.
Wrap other hand around finger.
Continue holding finger.
Link thumbs and flap hands so they resemble wings.

Jennifer Packard, West Bay Community Action, Warwick, RI

Butterfly Surprise

With this action rhyme, you can watch your little ones transform from caterpillars to butterflies!

First, I was a caterpillar crawling along,
Munching on leaves, and getting big and strong.
I made a cocoon; then I went to sleep.
I didn't move a muscle or make a peep!
When I woke up and opened my eyes,
I was a butterfly—what a surprise!

Wiggle on the floor.
Hold up arms and show off muscles.
Curl up in a ball.
Lie very still.
Open eyes and stretch.
Flap arms as if they are wings.

Kim Tyre, Mt. Calvary Preschool, Excelsior, MN

Crunch, Munch!
Leaves for Lunch!

Have each child make green fingerprints on a leaf cutout (pattern on page 42) so they resemble a caterpillar. Encourage him to draw antennae and facial details on his caterpillar. Then have him punch holes in the leaf. Mount a paper tree to a wall; then attach the leaves to the tree and title the display "Crunch, Munch! Leaves for Lunch!"

Amy Aloi, Bollman Bridge RECC, Jessup, MD

Our Creative Caterpillar!

Here's a unique display idea for youngsters' paintings! Mount finished paintings in a row. Then transform the paintings into a caterpillar by adding an enlarged head cutout from page 40 and several leg cutouts. Finally, title the display as shown.

Joanne Fusco, Tutor Time Child Care, Wappinger Falls, NY

These colorful yet tasty butterflies make a perfect snack.

To prepare for the snack:

- Collect the necessary ingredients and utensils using the lists on the recipe card below.
- Photocopy the step-by-step recipe cards on page 36.
- Color the cards; then cut them out and display them in the snack area.
- Follow the teacher preparation guidelines for the snack.

Bright Butterfly

Ingredients for one:
½ pretzel rod
pineapple ring
lemon yogurt
sprinkles

Utensils and supplies:
plastic bowl for each ingredient
small plastic spoon for each child
plastic knife for each child
disposable plate for each child

Teacher preparation:
Arrange the ingredients and supplies near the step-by-step recipe cards.

Beverly Carter
The Learning Center
Hagerstown, MD

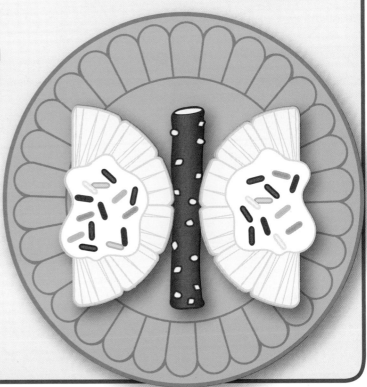

Recipe Cards

Use with "Bright Butterfly" on page 35.

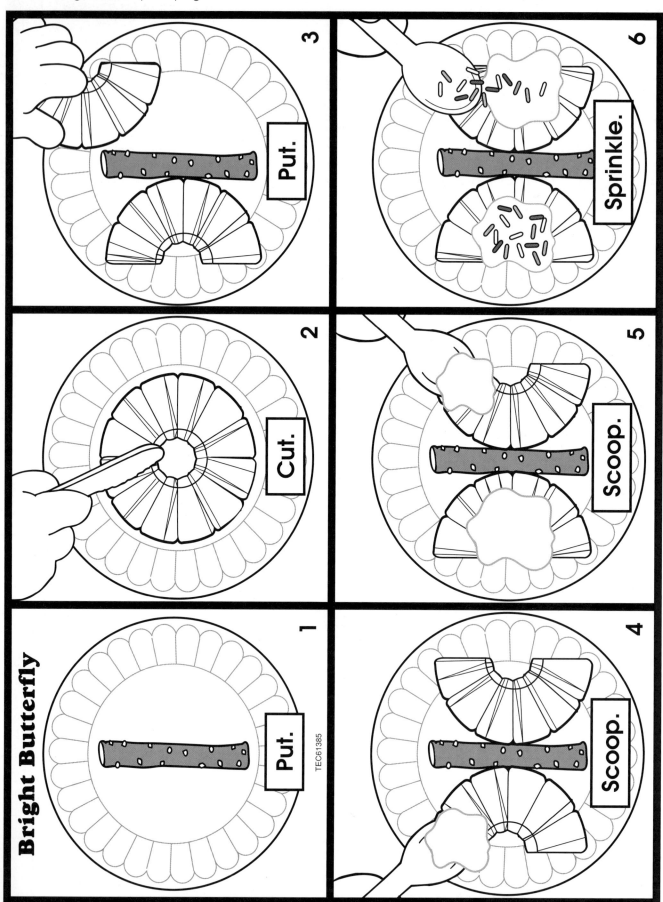

This tasty butterfly sandwich is the perfect snack.

To prepare for this snack:
- Collect the necessary ingredients and utensils using the lists on the recipe card below.
- Photocopy the step-by-step recipe cards on page 38.
- Color the cards; then cut them out and display them in the snack area.
- Follow the teacher preparation guidelines for the snack.

Beautiful Butterfly

Ingredients for one:
slice of bread
vegetable cream cheese
cucumber stick

Utensils and supplies:
disposable plate for each child
plastic knife for each child

Teacher Preparation:
Arrange the ingredients and supplies near the step-by-step recipe cards.

Melissa Rose
Early Childhood Alliance
Fort Wayne, IN

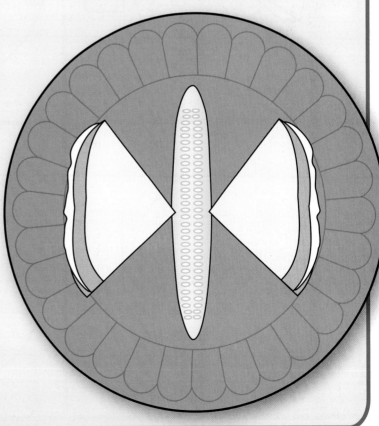

Recipe Cards

Use with "Beautiful Butterfly" on page 37.

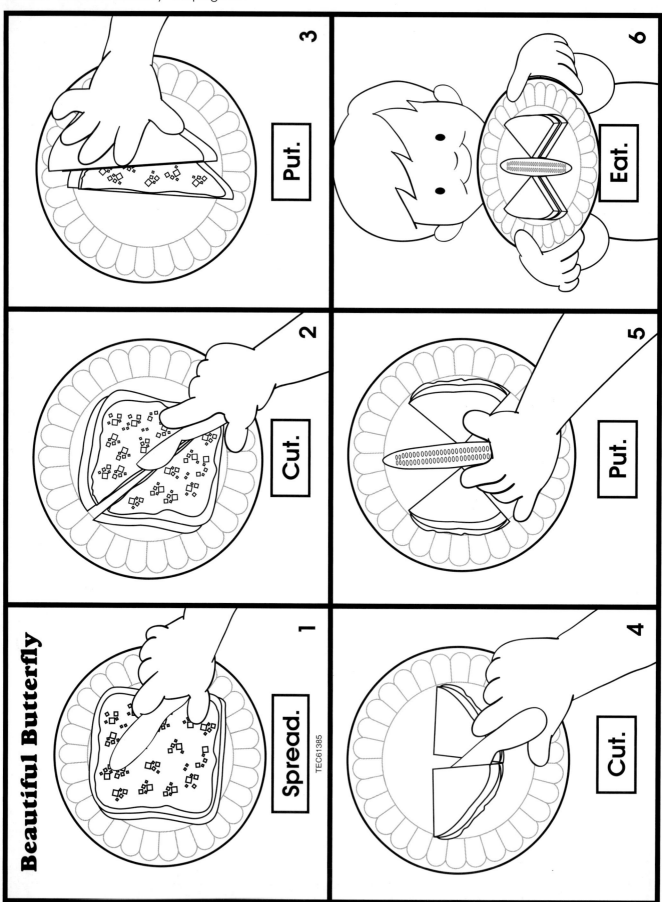

Dear Parent/Guardian,

We are making Bright Butterflies soon. We would be grateful if you could help by providing the following ingredient(s):

_____

_____

_____

We need the ingredient(s) listed above by _____.
date

Please let me know if you are able to send the ingredient(s).

Thank you,

_____
teacher

☐ Yes, I am able to send the ingredient(s).
☐ No, I am unable to send the ingredient(s) this time.

_____
parent/guardian signature

Dear Parent/Guardian,

We are making a Beautiful Butterfly Snack soon. We would be grateful if you could help by providing the following ingredient(s):

_____

_____

_____

We need the ingredient(s) listed above by _____.
date

Please let me know if you are able to send the ingredient(s).

Thank you,

_____
teacher

☐ Yes, I am able to send the ingredient(s).
☐ No, I am unable to send the ingredient(s) this time.

_____
parent/guardian signature

Caterpillar Head Pattern

Use with "A Colorful Caterpillar" on page 26 and "Our Creative Caterpillar" on page 34.

TEC61385

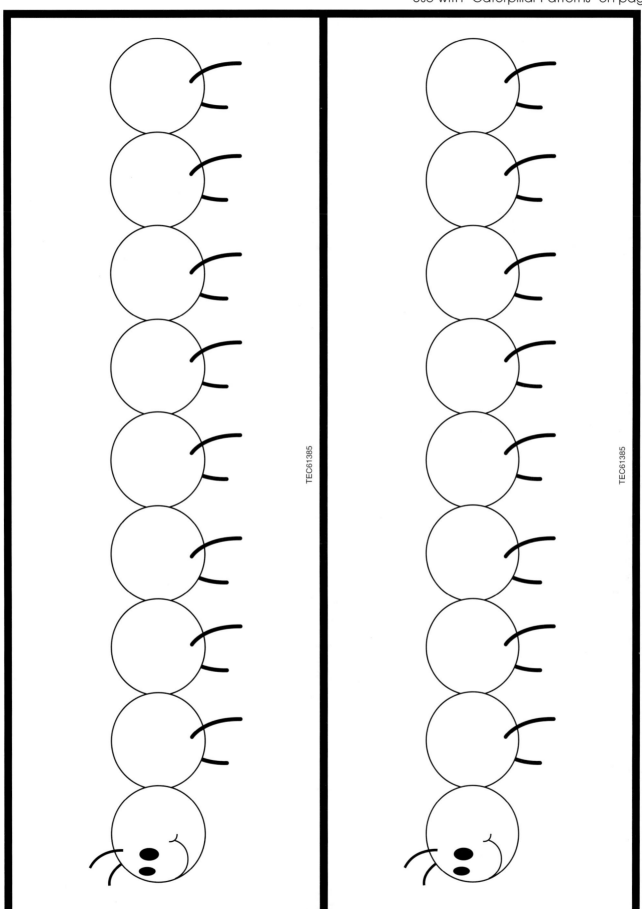

TEC61385

TEC61385

Leaf Patterns

Use with "Crunch, Munch! Leaves for Lunch!" on page 34.

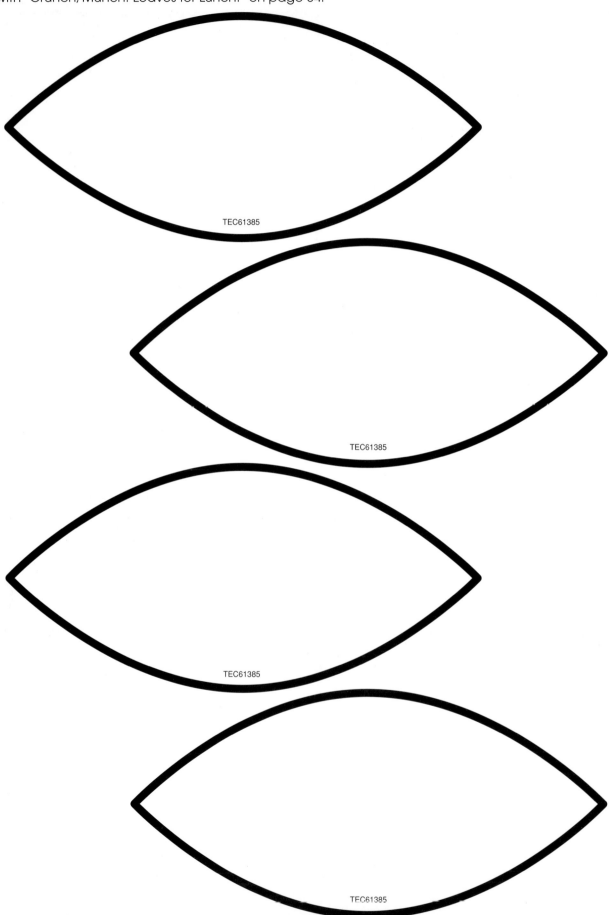

TEC61385

TEC61385

TEC61385

TEC61385

Butterfly Life Cycle Booklet

How to Use Pages 43–48

Use this booklet to help students learn about the life cycle of a butterfly. Give each child a copy of pages 44, 45, 46, and 47. Read aloud the text on the booklet cover and pages as you help youngsters follow the directions below.

Directions for Each Student

1. Booklet cover: write your name.
2. Cut out the picture cards from page 47.
3. Booklet pages 1–3: glue the corresponding picture card to each page.
4. Booklet page 4: color the butterfly.
5. Booklet page 5: trace the dotted lines to review the life cycle of a butterfly.
6. Cut out the booklet cover and pages. (Make sure to cut around the butterfly on page 4, keeping it attached to the page.) Fold the butterfly forward.
7. Stack the cover and the booklet pages in order; then staple them together on the left side.

Finished Sample

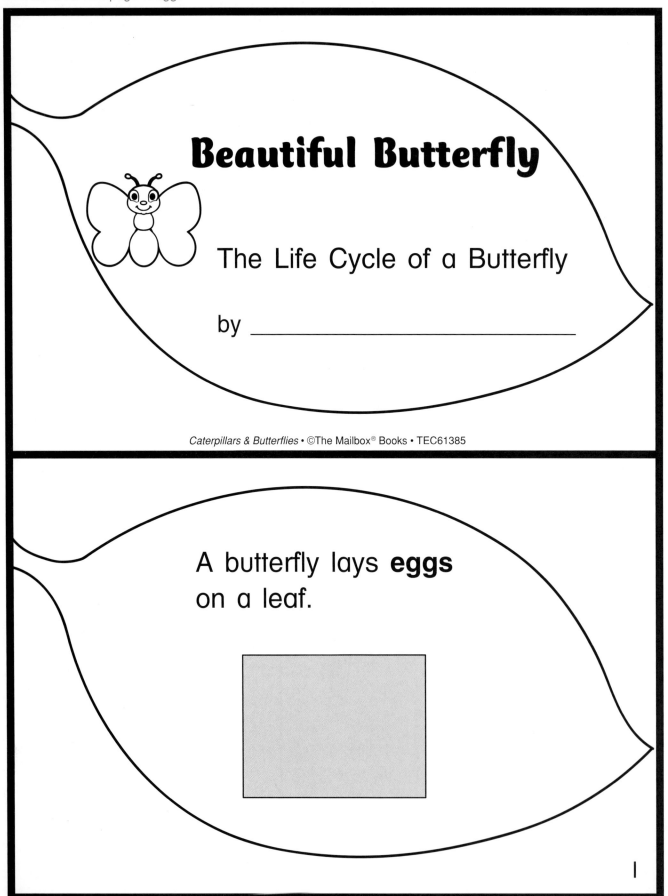

Beautiful Butterfly

The Life Cycle of a Butterfly

by _____

Caterpillars & Butterflies • ©The Mailbox® Books • TEC61385

A butterfly lays **eggs** on a leaf.

1

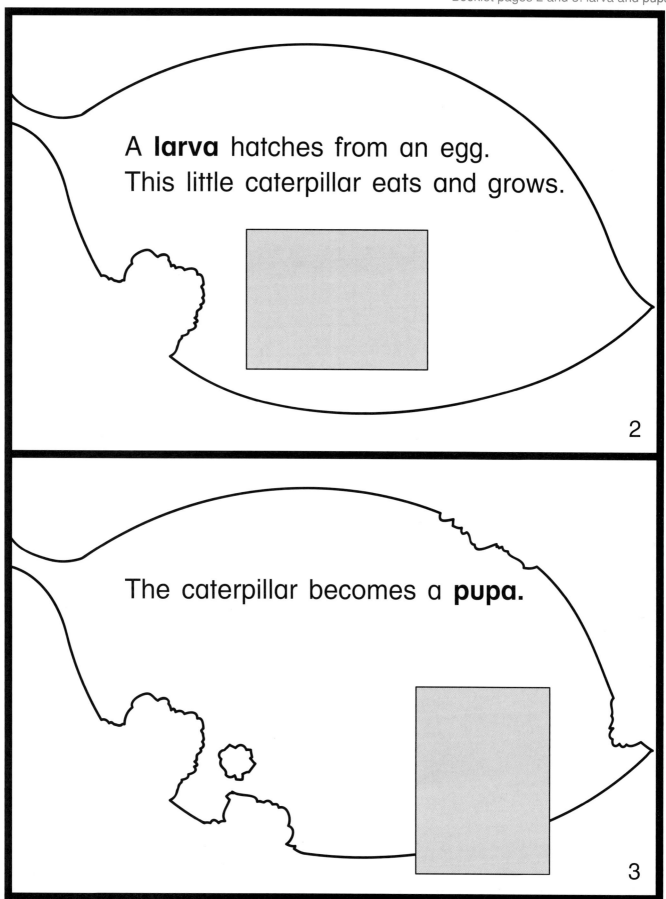

A **larva** hatches from an egg.
This little caterpillar eats and grows.

2

The caterpillar becomes a **pupa.**

3

Fold here.

Out comes a **butterfly!**

4

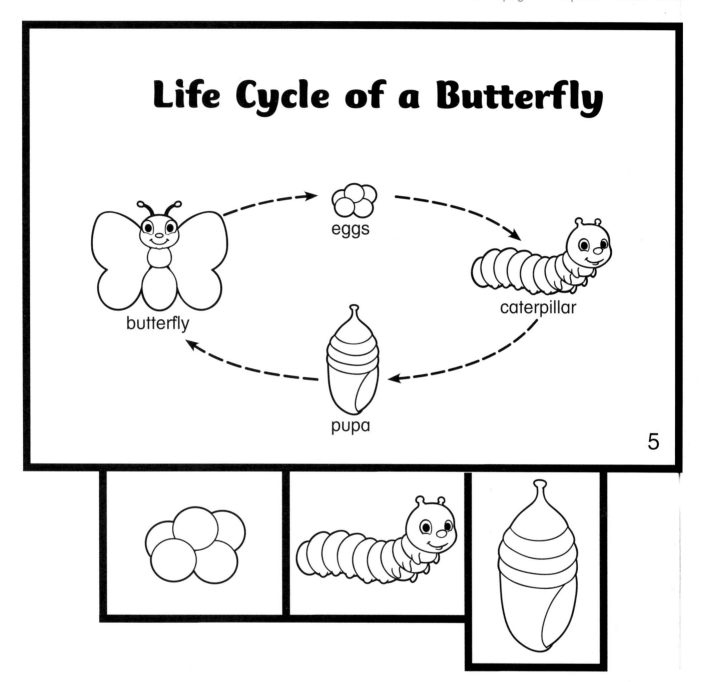

Life Cycle of a Butterfly

eggs

caterpillar

butterfly

pupa

5

Use with "Life Cycle of a Butterfly" on pages 44 and 45.

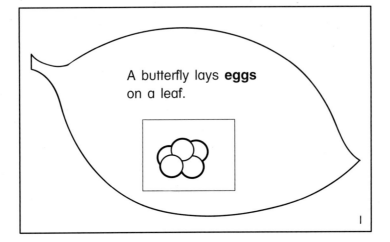

A butterfly lays **eggs** on a leaf.

1

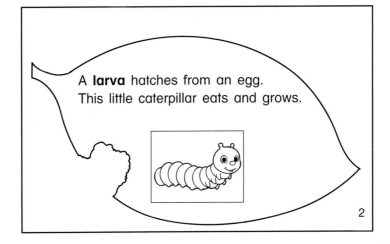

A **larva** hatches from an egg. This little caterpillar eats and grows.

2

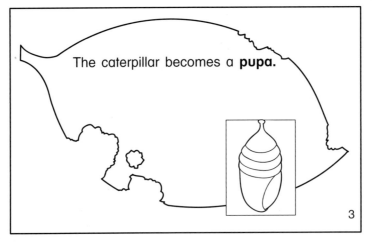

The caterpillar becomes a **pupa.**

3